CALIFORNIA
WILDERNESS COAST
JOHN FIELDER

Photography and Words
by John Fielder

California Littlebooks

Westcliffe Publishers, Inc. Englewood, Colorado

First frontispiece: Clearing fog, Sonoma County coast

Second frontispiece: Evening light, San Mateo County coast

Third frontispiece: Indian paintbrush wildflowers, Big Sur, Monterey County

Opposite: Surf and fog, Sonoma County coast

International Standard Book Number:
ISBN 0-942394-26-7
Library of Congress Catalogue Card Number:
86-050068
Copyright: John Fielder, 1986
Designer: Gerald Miller Simpson/Denver
Typographer: Edward A. Nies
Printer: Dai Nippon Printing Company, Ltd.
              Tokyo, Japan
Publisher: Westcliffe Publishers, Inc.
              P.O. Box 1261
              Englewood, Colorado 80150-1261

PREFACE

Two years of my life were occupied photographing, what is to me, the most diverse landscape in one single state. Though I live in Colorado, a very scenic state itself, I always had a desire to see and photograph California. Not only does it offer mountains, but it contains some of our country's most beautiful deserts, and many miles of spectacular coastline.

I enjoyed my hikes and photographic forays into the Sierra Nevada Range of California very much. They offer scenery that is unique to any in Colorado and other parts of the Rockies. I also derived great pleasure from experiencing the deserts of the Mohave and the Anza-Borrego State Park. The landscape there challenged me to become more perceptive with my eyes. I also enjoyed photographing all of the places in between these major domains. It was fun to watch green hills of winter turn golden in summer, and to see the magnificent oak trees that decorate the state from one end to the other.

However, I think I most enjoyed seeing for the first time the coastline of the Pacific Ocean. It is more different from what I had been used to in Colorado than any other domain I saw in California; and it challenged my creativity with the camera more than the other domains. The ocean and its interaction with the land is a very dynamic affair, and my ability to react quickly to changing conditions was tested. The weather is constantly changing, too, and this was another test of my perspicacity.

In two years I hiked and drove the Pacific coast in California from Santa Barbara to the Oregon border about four full times. In that time I was able to see the same places under different atmospheric conditions, and more importantly, in different conditions of light. I also experienced the coast during all of the seasons, through which colors and floral growth change dramatically.

The photographs in this book are a few of my favorite images of the California wilderness coast. Though there are no legally designated "wilderness areas" along the California coast, as there are in Washington state's Olympic Park, much of this land is still very pristine. With the unyielding work of the Pacific Ocean, it's no wonder. Even when near developed areas, the immediate land at the edge of the ocean, usually the wildest, is often unblemished. The only scar is the debris that washes up on shore from sea.

Evening light isolates shapes of the rugged coast, Sonoma County

Though I photographed the entire coast, except the area south of Santa Barbara to Mexico where there is entirely too much development, I concentrated upon certain regions. One of my favorites was Big Sur. Located in Monterey County, it is a precipitous area with steep cliffs falling straight into the ocean. There are relatively few access points to the beaches, where there are beaches. Where there is access, the scenery is dramatic; and the views from Highway 1 are some of the most awesome in the state.

I also spent a great deal of time between Santa Cruz and San Francisco. In between these two points are great long stretches of sand and giant red cliffs. The Ana Nuevo Reserve has beautiful dunes and unique coastline. And when in season, the artichokes are the best in the world!

The coast from San Francisco north to the Oregon border is spectacular all of the way. I was especially aroused by the rugged, rocky beaches in Sonoma County. The sea stacks penetrate the ocean in great numbers here, and the pebbly beaches are colorful and fun on which to walk. Here in May the wildflowers are especially fecund.

The coast just north and south of Eureka is unique to any other in the state. The broad beaches are lined with the remains of trees swept from the forests during winter storms, and lost from logging operations. The surf is rugged all year, the winds often blow hard, and the gray beaches are very photogenic.

To some of the photographs I have written poems that evoke feelings that I experienced when at that location. I remember the emotion that I felt when I was there, the conditions of weather, and something in particular that remained as a thought about the place after I left. Together, the words and photographs are my personal way of manifesting my experiences while traveling the magnificent wilderness coast of California.

John Fielder

This ancient rock it seems to say
Along on my top you're free to play
To walk along my edge all day
Have lunch, relax, I hope you'll stay

Ana Nuevo State Reserve, San
Mateo County

One evening o'er the beach I roam
Across I came so much sea foam
It isn't what it looks I hope
A patch of wayward laundry soap

Sea foam, Trinidad Beach,
Humboldt County

Overleaf: Evening light, Big Sur, Monterey County

The mist is thick and all around
It lays small drops of water down
Through the lens I barely see
Wet beauty here beside the sea

High tide approaches, Big Sur,
Monterey County

For life along the ocean's edge
From shells to kelp and marine sedge
Sea water is a shiny garnish
For me there is no better varnish

Brown algae, Monterey County coast

Awash they are with fallen wood
The shores perhaps they'd say we should
Not use the sea to dump debris
For cleaner would these waters be

Cape Mendocino, Humboldt County

Overleaf: Lupine fields, Pt. Reyes

I guess it may be hard to tell
That o'er the edge I almost fell
The winds were fierce on this clear day
And with me nearly had their way

Big Sur, Monterey County

Morning light's my greatest joy
For with it cameras are a toy
Great colors here they do reflect
Fine photographs I would expect

Low tide, Mendocino County coast

The joy of being on the coast
Is something I enjoy the most
It should be clear from this one scene
To me just what the coast does mean

Eel-grass colors the Sonoma County coast

Overleaf: Shell beach is bludgeoned by the surf, Sonoma County

Great journeys did we have to take
And on this beach we made our stake
Though tons we weigh we are not sure
How long a stay we will endure

Driftwood, Humboldt County coast

So smooth they are the sea is strong
It grinds away it won't take long
For these great rocks that now are tall
They one day will be rendered small

Sonoma County coast

Overleaf: Driftwood at Patrick's Point, Humboldt County

Just how it came here I can't guess
It's out of place I must confess
I tried my best to use restraint
To see if I could scratch the paint

Shell Beach, Sonoma County coast

If wilderness to you does call
And if you wish to see it all
Remember not to look too far
Beneath your feet are great things small

Brown algae, Big Sur, Monterey County

One great thing about the coast
A thing I think I like the most
The fog that starts before the day
Soon turns to clouds above the bay

Mendocino County coast

Though fog is great for moody scenes
For clear days, too, I'm often keen
I sometimes tire of being moist
Beneath the sun I do rejoice

Big Sur, Monterey County

A trick I've played upon your view
I think an explanation's due
O'er ten seconds was this scene shot
A single wave is what it's not

Dusk on the Sonoma County coast

Overleaf: Pt. Delgada, Humboldt County

It seems that water has a plan
To find a way through all that sand
But if it was just up to me
I'd pick a line straight to the sea

Big Sur, Monterey County

Overleaf: Flowers of wild mustard, Pt. Reyes, Marin County

Greens and browns are all around
Plants this color do abound
On cloudy days they tend to make
Great scenes for me to find and take

Sonoma County coast

In evening when the sun does fall
Along the coast out on the capes
All rocks that stand out from the cliffs
The shadows carve them into shapes

Big Sur, Mendocino County

In Spring the flowers love to drink
From coastal fog they're on the brink
Of being washed way out to sea
Perhaps a place they'd like to be

Lupine wildflowers in May, Sonoma
County coast

The surf below is very white
Especially from this lofty height
It's white because the wind is strong
Big waves don't last for very long

Pt. Reyes, Marin County